GUIDE TO IMPROVING YOUR GRAMMAR

THE EASYWAY

Robert Fry

Easyway Guides

© Straightforward Publishing 2013

British Cataloguing in Publication data. A catalogue record is available for this book from the British Library.

ISBN 9871847163523

Printed in the United Kingdom by Berforts Press
Cover design by Straightforward Graphics

Whilst every effort has been made to ensure that the information in this book is accurate at the time of going to print, the author and publisher recognise that the information can become out of date. The book is therefore sold on the understanding that no responsibility for errors and omissions is assumed and no responsibility is held for the information held within.

Contents

Introduction

Section one- English Language and Grammar

Section 2-Practical English usage

Introduction

Many people struggle with the basic rules of English Grammar, indeed many people prefer not to know the rules of grammar, as the subject is complicated and doesn't seem to make a lot of sense most of the time. Why bother with grammar when you can just carry on regardless and get by with what you know?

The answer is that you will need to bother with grammar in the world of work, depending on your job. You will need to know how to write reports and letters and also to fill in forms. On a fundamental level, you will need to know how to express yourself correctly in order to further yourself. Essentially, knowledge of the rules of grammar and how to apply them will greatly empower you and will improve your self confidence.

It is true to say that many people miss out altogether on English Grammar at school and, in later life wished that they hadn't. The main point of this book is to introduce the person who is interested to the basic rules of grammar and to develop this into practical everyday use. In We start with sentence construction and then develop the main rules of grammar, Verbs, Nouns, Adjectives, Adverbials, Clauses and Prepositions.

In chapter 8 we will explore the effective use of punctuation, in chapter 9 we look at spelling and in the second section we look at applying the lessons learnt in the first section to practical everyday use, such as writing an essay or short story, writing a business or personal letter and finally writing a CV or application form.

1
Sentences and Parts of Sentences

In this chapter we will look at sentences and parts of sentences, before leading onto the main elements of English Grammar.

Sentences

Although it might seem obvious, sentences are made up of words. Sentences can consist of any number of words which can be configured in a number of ways.

They went out
The woman on the railway station had a cup of coffee
Whatever I do, I am very self-conscious
Well, see you then.

There are many ways to put words together to construct sentences:

We can do this
Can we do this?

Grammar describes the way we put words together. Each word in a particular sentence belongs to a particular set or **class**, depending on how they are used. These particular classes are known as **parts of speech.**

All sentences, irrespective, will begin with a capital letter and end in either a full stop or a question mark or exclamation mark. These particular marks are known as punctuation, which we will elaborate on further in this book.

The term clause describes a group of words that contains a **verb** (see next chapter), the **subject** of that verb and also, some other words such as an **object.**

A sentence can contain one or more **Clauses.**

They will assist you **if you will allow them**
If you need to see something,, just drop in and see if I am here

Many sentences are made up of a single clause, which are called **simple** sentences.

They arrived last Sunday
Peter adores his cat.

A clause will always contain a verb, which can be known as a **doing word** so called because verbs describe actions (see next chapter).

Run   Think
Walk   Skip

A sentence does not always have to be a clause (see further on for more about clauses)

Certainly not
Yes
Why?

A phrase is just a group of words. The term 'phrase' is usually kept for words which naturally go together.

My friend Susan
Should have been running
Over there

Many words can refer to either one thing only or to more than one thing. The terms **singular** and **plural** are used for this. A more general term is **number.** When we wish to identify the speaker or the person referred to in grammar, we use what is known as the **first person,** to mean the speaker, the **second person** to mean the person who is being spoken to, and the **third person** to mean the person who is being spoken about. For example, we talk about the 'first person plural' or the 'third person singular'.

A **verb** tells about an action or state of being. Ordinary verbs are called **main verbs** - *Come go want believe*

As stated above, a main verb is more commonly known as a 'doing word'. This is the simplest way to remember the meaning of a verb. A special group of verbs are known as auxiliary verbs. these can be put together with main verbs to form different tenses.

I **am** walking
I **can** assist you
We **might** have to

A **noun** (see Chapter 3) is a word that labels a thing or an idea. Nouns are sometimes known as **naming** words.

Fence   Table   Time   Animal

If we do not want to repeat the same noun in a sentence or a paragraph we can replace it with a **pronoun**. A pronoun is a word that is used instead of a noun phrase or a noun.

*David saw Peter so **he** asked **him** to assist him*

An adjective gives more information about a noun. Adjectives help us describe or pick out which particular thing among many is being referred to. Adjectives are sometimes called '**describing words**'.

*A woman The **big** man Their **new** radio The dog The cat*

A **determiner** is used to point more precisely to the person, thing or idea that is being talked about. examples of determiners are **definite** and **indefinite** articles and **possessives.**

The dog My uncle Their radio

An **adverb** (see Chapter 4) gives information about the way that an action is carried out or when and where it takes place.

He fled **quickly** down the riverbank
She raised the case **slowly**

A **preposition** (see Chapter 7)
is one of a small group of words that can be used with nouns and verbs. Prepositions give information about position or movement.

On the bank   Over the path   In the evening

When a preposition is used in front of a noun, the two together do the work of an adverb.

*He is coming **now***
*he is coming **in the morning***
*I found him **there***

A **conjunction**, as its name suggests, joins two or more nouns or clauses to each other. Conjunctions are sometimes known as 'joining words'.

*He went to the library **and** took out a book*

*I took out a book **but** forgot to take one back*

Parts of the sentence

A sentence consists of a number of parts, using different parts of speech. the most important parts of speech are:

- The **subject**, which is either a noun phrase or a pronoun (see further on). Normally the subject comes before the verb phrase in a sentence.

*The **boys** had been climbing*

*The **new tutor** arrived*

***They** had finished*

- The **verb phrase**, which includes the main verb and which may have auxiliary verbs to go with it (see further on)

*The boys **had been climbing***

*The new tutor **arrived***

*They **had finished***

- The **object,** which is a noun phrase or a pronoun

*He used his **bike***

*Dave was reading a new **book***
*Raymond discovered **it***

- An **adverbial** or **adjunct**

This may be:

- a single word, an adverb.

Suddenly, it started to snow **heavily**

- an **adverbial** phrase, a group of words that functions as an adverb

In the evening, *the moon was clear*
*You wont see it **after a while***

-an **adverbial clause**, a group of words including a verb, which functions as an adverb.

*I'll get some sandwiches for you **when I've poured the tea**.*
***When I've poured the tea**, I'll get some sandwiches for you.*

- A **complement.** With certain verbs, such as be and seem, a complement takes the place of an object. A complement can either be an adjective or a noun phrase.

*He became **a teacher** in 2009*
*Dave is a **plumber***
*He felt **rather silly** when he realised his mistake*

In this chapter we have looked at sentences and parts of sentences and have been briefly introduced to the main elements of English Grammar. In Chapters 2-9 we will expand on each of these elements. In the next chapter, we will look at the first of the main elements, **verbs.**

****

2

More About Grammar-The use of Verbs

Having discussed the nature of sentences and sentence parts, it is now time to take a more in-depth look at verbs.

Verbs are a class of words used to show the performance of an action (do, throw, run), existence (be), possession (have), or state (know, love) of a subject.

To put it simply a verb shows what something or someone does.

Most statements in speech and writing have a main verb. These verbs are expressed in tenses which place everything in a point in time.

Verbs have **moods**, which indicate the viewpoint of the verb, whether it is a fact, a command or hypothetical.

Verbs also have a **voice**. The voice shows whether the subject of a sentence is carrying out an action, or is having an action carried out on it.

Verbs are conjugated (inflected) to reflect how they are used. There are two general areas in which conjugation occurs; for person and for tense. Conjugation for tense is carried out on all verbs. All conjugations start with the infinitive form of the verb. The infinitive is simply the *to* form of the verb, for example, *to begin*. The present participle form (the -ing form), is formed by adding *ing* to the bare infinitive. For example, the present participle of the verb *to begin* is *beginning*. There are two other forms that the verb can take, depending on the tense type and time, the simple past form (*began*) and the past participle (*begun*). The first person occurs when the verb changes form, depending on whether it is governed by a first, second, or third person subject.

Action Verbs

Action verbs are verbs that show the performance of an action. they are dynamic verbs that show something happening.

There are regular and irregular action verbs. For example:

- To walk is a regular action verb
- To run is an irregular action verb

Regular Verbs Simple Past / Past Participle Spelling Rules

The simple past tense is formed by adding -ed to the end of the verb. However there are several rules depending on the spelling of the verb, these are:-

If the base of the verb ends in:-

- -e only add -d (raid - raided)
- a consonant plus -y the y is turned into -ied (study - studied / try -tried)
- -c add -ked (panic - panicked)
- a single vowel plus a consonant and is stressed on its final syllable the consonant is usually doubled and -ed added (plan - planned)
- -p, g or -m the consonant is usually doubled and -ed added (ram - rammed / tap - tapped / gag - gagged)
- -l the consonant is usually doubled (travel - travelled)

Auxiliary (Helping) Verbs

Auxiliary means functioning in a supporting capacity, and that is exactly what these auxiliary verbs do, which is why they are also known as helping verbs. They are used together with a main verb to give grammatical information and therefore add extra meaning to a sentence

Be, Do and Have are auxiliary verbs, they are irregular verbs and can be used as main verbs. The verbs 'to be' and 'to have' are the most commonly used auxiliary verbs and work alongside the main verbs in any statement.

Be

Be is the most common verb in the English language. It can be used as an auxiliary and a main verb. It is used a lot in its other forms.

19

Base form = *be*

Present form = *am/is/are*

Past form = *was/were*

Present Participle / Gerund = *being*

Past Participle = *been*

Do

The verb **do** is one of the most common verbs in English. It can be used as an auxiliary and a main verb. It is often used in questions.

Base form = *do*

Present form = *do/does*

Past form = *did*

Present Participle / Gerund = *doing*

Past Participle = *done*

Have

Have is one of the most common verbs in the English language.

Base form = *have*

Present form = *have / has*

Past form = *had*

Present Participle / Gerund = *having*

Past Participle = *had*

Irregular verbs

Irregular verbs have no rules for conjugation. These can only be learnt in context. They all have a base form. *e.g. to run*

A gerund (ing) form where *ing* is added to the end of the verb. *e.g. running*

An -s form where *s* is added to the end of the verb. *e.g. runs*

A past tense form which must be learnt. *e.g. ran*

A past participle form which must be learnt. *e.g. run*

The Main Verb

Sometimes there is more than one kind of verb in a sentence. There are auxiliary verbs, modal verbs, and main verbs (sometimes called full or non-auxiliary verbs).

The main verb expresses the main action or state of being of the subject in the sentence and changes form according to the subject (singular, plural, 1st person, 2nd person, 3rd person).

Most statements in speech and writing have a main verb.

The main verb changes its form according to the verb form (perfect tense, past tense, simple tense etc).

For example:

- Dogs usually chase cats.
- But my cat chases my dog.
- My cat is chasing my dog.
- My dog has sometimes chased my cat.
- But, only because my cat ate my dog's dinner.
- My cat has been eating my dog's dinner a lot.

Mood

Verbs have moods, not good moods and bad moods though, they're not actually moody, here 'mood' (sometimes 'mode') comes from the Latin for 'manner'. The so called mood of the verb simply expresses the viewpoint of the speaker or writer; their wishes, intents, or assertions about reality.

In English there are three moods:-

The indicative mood is the most common one; it is used to state facts, to deny things, or ask a question.

The imperative mood is used to give commands.

The least used mood, but the one that gives people the most trouble, is the subjunctive mood. The subjunctive mood is usually used to express doubt or show that a situation is hypothetical

What is a Phrasal Verb?

A phrasal verb is a combination of a verb and preposition, a verb and an adverb, or a verb with both an adverb and a preposition. A phrasal verb has a meaning which is different from the original verb. That's what makes them fun, but confusing. You may need to try to guess the meaning from the context, or, failing that, look it up in a dictionary.

The adverb or preposition that follows the verb are sometimes called a particle. The particle changes the meaning of the phrasal verb in idiomatic ways. Phrasal verbs are usually used informally in everyday speech as opposed to the more formal Latinate verbs, such as "to get together" rather than "to congregate", "to put off" rather than "to postpone", or "to get out" rather than "to exit". They should be avoided in academic writing.

Literal usage

Many verbs in English can be combined with an adverb or a preposition, a phrasal verb used in a literal sense with a preposition is easy to understand.

- "He *walked across* the square.

Verb and adverb constructions are also easy to understand when used literally.

- "He opened the shutters and *looked outside.*"
- "When she heard the crash, she *looked up.*"

An adverb in a literal phrasal verb modifies the verb it is attached to, and a preposition links the subject to the verb.

Regular Verbs

Regular verbs are conjugated to easy to learn rules.

They all have a base form. *e.g. to look*

A gerund (ing) form where *ing* is added to the end of the verb. *e.g. looking*

An -s form where *s* is added to the end of the verb. *e.g. looks*

A past tense form where *ed* is added to the end of the verb. *e.g. looked* (Click here for the spelling rules)

A past participle form where *ed* is added to the end of the verb. *e.g. looked* (Click here for the spelling rules).

Stative verbs are verbs that show a state and not an action.

You can group verbs that show a state in the following ways:-

Verbs that show thought - believe, doubt, know, understand etc. Verbs that show possession - have, own, want, contain etc. Verbs that show senses - hear, see, smell etc. Verbs that show emotion - love, hate, want, need etc.

There are regular and irregular stative verbs. But when they are used to show a particular state they do not take the -ing form. For Example:

- I like pork pies (Never "I am liking...")
- I know a lot of Spanish words. (Never "I am knowing...")

However, some verbs can be used to show an action or a state.

For Example:

- I think French is easy. = It is my opinion.
- I'm thinking of joining a new course. = I am considering it.

In this chapter we have looked at a main element of English Grammar, the Verb. At first, verbs may seem complicated as there is a lot to remember but the more that you study them the more that they make sense.

In chapter 3, we will look at another main element of English Grammar, the **Noun,**

3

The Use of Nouns

A **noun** is the word that refers to a person, thing or abstract idea. A noun can tell you who or what.

The meaning of 'Nouns'. What is a Noun?

- There are several different types of noun:- There are common nouns such as **dog, car, chair etc.**
- Nouns that refer to things which can be counted (can be singular or plural) are **Countable nouns** .
- Nouns that refer to some groups of countable nouns, substances, feelings and types of activity (can only be singular) are **Uncountable nouns.**
- Nouns that refer to a group of people or things are **Collective nouns.**
- Nouns that refer to people, organisations or places are **Proper nouns**, only proper nouns are capitalised.
- Nouns that are made up of two or more words are called **Compound nouns.**
- Nouns that are formed from a verb by adding *-ing* are called **Gerunds**

- A **Common noun** is a word that names people, places, things, or ideas. They are not the names of a single person, place or thing.
- A common noun begins with a lowercase letter unless it is at the beginning of a sentence. For example
- **People:-**
- man, girl, boy, mother, father, child, person, teacher, student
- **Animals:-**
- cat, dog, fish, ant, snake
- **Things:-**
- book, table, chair, phone
- **Places:-**
- school, city, building, shop
- **Ideas:-**
- love, hate, idea, pride

A noun can be **countable** or **uncountable.** Countable nouns can be "counted", they have a singular and plural form . For example:

- A book, two books, three books .....
- An apple, two apples, three apples ....

Uncountable nouns (also called mass nouns or noncount nouns) cannot be counted, they are not separate objects. This means you cannot make them plural by adding -s, because they only have a singular form. It also means that they do not take a/an or a number in front of them. For example:

- Water
- Work
- Information
- Coffee
- Sand

What is a collective noun?

A collective noun is a noun that can be singular in form whilst referring to a group of people or things. Collective nouns are sometimes confused with mass nouns.

Groups of people - army, audience, band, choir, class, committee, crew, family, gang, jury, orchestra, police, staff, team, trio

Groups of animals - colony, flock, herd, pack, pod, school, swarm

Groups of things - bunch, bundle, clump, pair, set, stack

The use of "of" -We often say a group *of* things, such as a bunch of flowers, or a host of golden daffodils.

Some collective nouns can stand alone, such as "Britain has an army", but if the collective noun "army" is used to mean something other than an organized military force, you can say things like "an army of women" or "an army of ants", and even "an army of one".

Plural or singular?

When a group is considered as a single unit, the collective noun is used with a singular verb and singular pronoun. For example - *The committee has reached its decision.*

When the focus is on the individual parts of the group, British English sometimes uses a plural verb and plural pronouns.

For example - *"The committee have been arguing all morning."* This is the same as saying "*The people in the committee have been ...."*

However, if you are talking about more than one committee, then you use the plural form.

For example - "*Many committees have been formed over the years.*"

A determiner in front of a singular collective noun is always singular: *this committee* , never *these committee* (but of course when the collective noun is pluralized, it takes a plural determiner: *these committees*).

Proper nouns (also called proper names) are the words which name specific people, organisations or places. They always start with a capital letter. For example:-

Each part of a person's name is a proper noun:-

David Davies – Fiona Cann Rupert Smith ...

The names of companies, organisations or trade marks:-

Ford - Suzuki - the Round Table - WWW

Given or pet names of animals:-

Fido Trigger Sam

The names of cities and countries and words derived from those proper nouns:-

Paris - London - New York - England - English

Geographical and Celestial Names:-

the Red Sea - Alpha Centauri - Mars

Monuments, buildings, meeting rooms:-

The Taj Mahal - The Eiffel Tower - Room 222

Historical events, documents, laws, and periods:-

the Civil War - the Industrial Revolution - World War I

Months, days of the week, holidays:-

Monday - Christmas - December

Religions, deities, scriptures:-

God - Christ - Jehovah - Christianity - Judaism - Islam - the Bible - the Koran - the Torah

Awards, vehicles, vehicle models and names, brand names:-

the Nobel Peace Prize - the Scout Movement - Ford Focus - the *Bismarck* - Kleenex - Hoover

A compound noun is a noun that is made up of two or more words. Most compound nouns in English are formed by nouns modified by other nouns or adjectives.

The words *tooth* and *paste* are each nouns in their own right, but if you join them together they form a new word - *toothpaste*. The word *black* is an adjective and *board* is a noun, but if you join them together they form a new word - *blackboard*. In both these example the first word modifies or describes the second word, telling us what kind of object or person it is, or what its purpose is. A **gerund** (often known as an -ing word) is a noun formed from a verb by adding *-ing*. It can follow a preposition, adjective and most often another verb.

For example:

- I enjoy *walking.*

An abstract noun is a noun that you cannot sense, it is the name we give to an emotion, ideal or idea. They have no physical existence, you can't see, hear, touch, smell or taste them. The opposite of an abstract noun is a concrete noun.

For example:-

Justice; an idea, bravery and happiness are all abstract nouns

In this chapter, we have looked briefly at Nouns. In chapter 4, we will explore **adjectives.**

4

The Use of Adjectives

> **Adjectives** describe or give information about nouns or pronouns.
>
> For example:-
>
> The *black* dog barked. (The adjective *black* describes the noun "*dog*".)

The good news is that the form of an adjective does not change. It does not matter if the noun being modified is male or female, singular or plural, subject or object.

Some adjectives give us factual information about the noun - age, size colour etc. Some adjectives show what somebody thinks about something or somebody - nice, horrid, beautiful etc (opinion adjectives - not everyone may agree).

If you are asked questions with which, whose, what kind, or how many, you need an adjective to be able to answer.

There are different types of adjectives in the English language:

- Numeric: six, one hundred and one
- Quantitative: more, all, some, half, more than enough
- Qualitative: colour, size, smell etc.
- Possessive: my, his, their, your
- Interrogative: which, whose, what
- Demonstrative: this, that, those, these

Opinion

Adjectives can be used to give your opinion about something.

good, pretty, right, wrong, funny, light, happy, sad, full, soft, hard etc.

For example:

He was a *pretty* boy.

Size

Adjectives can be used to describe size.

big, small, little, long, tall, short, same as, etc.

For example:

- "The big man." or "The big woman".

Age

Adjectives can be used to describe *age.*

For example:

- "He was an *old* man. " or "She was an *old* woman."

Shape

Adjectives can be used to describe ***shape***.

round, circular, triangular, rectangular, square, oval, etc.

For example:

- "It was a *square* box. " or "They were *square* boxes."

Colour

Adjectives can be used to describe colour.

blue, red, green, brown, yellow, black, white, etc.

For example:

- "The blue bag." or "The blue bags".

Origin

Adjectives can be used to describe origin.

For example:-

- "It was a *German* flag." or "They were *German* flags."

Material

Adjectives can be used to identify the *material* something is made of.

- "A *wooden* cupboard." or *"Wooden* cupboards."

Distance

Adjectives can be used to describe *distance*.

long, short, far, around, start, high, low, etc.

For example:

- "She went for a *long* walk." or "She went for lots of *long* walks."

Temperature

Adjectives can be used to describe *temperature*.

cold, warm, hot, cool, etc.

For example:

- "The day was *hot.*" or "The days were *hot.*"

Time

Adjectives can be used to describe *time*.

late, early, bed, nap, dinner, lunch, day, morning, night, etc.

For example:

- "She had an *early* start."

Purpose

Adjectives can be used to describe *purpose. (These adjectives often end with "-ing".)*

For example:

- "She gave them a *sleeping bag.* " or 'She gave them *sleeping* bags."

When using more than one adjective to modify a noun, the adjectives may be separated by a conjunction (and) or by commas (,).

For example:

- "Her hair was long and blonde." or "She had long, blonde hair."

Adjectives can also be used after some verbs. They do not describe the verb, adverbs do that. Adjectives after a verb describe the subject of the verb (usually a noun or pronoun). They are called predicative adjectives.

For example:

- "David looks tired." The subject (in this case David) is being described as tired not the verb *to look.*

Adjectives can be used to describe lots of things, from physical size, age, shape, colour, material, to more abstract things like opinion, origin and purpose. We can use adjectives together to give a detailed description of something. Adjectives that express opinions usually come before all others, but it can sometimes depend on what exactly you want to emphasise.

For example:

"That nice, big, blue bag." (You like the bag.)
"That big, nice, blue bag." (You like the colour.)

Possessive adjectives
Possessive adjectives are used to show ownership or possession.

Subject pronoun	Possessive adjective
I	my
you	your
he	his
she	her
it	its
we	our
they	their

For example:

- I own a laptop. = It is *my* laptop.
- You own this computer (I presume). = It is *your* computer.
- My husband owns a car. = It is *his* car.
- My sister owns a house. = It is *her* house.
- My dog owns a collar. = It is *its* collar.
- We use this website. = It is *our* website.
- Manchester United own a football ground. = It is *their* football ground

---

In this chapter, we have explored adjectives. In chapter 5, we will look at **adverbials.**

5

The Use of Adverbials

> **Adverbials** modify or tell us something about the sentence or the verb. It may be a single adverb, a phrase, or a prepositional phrase, or a clause element.

When an adverbial modifies a verb, it changes the meaning of that verb.

For example:-

The teachers at me.
The teachers looked at me **anxiously**. *(The verb* **looked** *suddenly has a very different meaning).*

When an adverbial modifies a sentence, the meaning of the sentence changes.

For example:-

I failed all of my exams.
Surprisingly, *I failed all of my exams.*

Word groups that are also considered to be adverbials can also modify verbs: a prepositional phrase, a noun phrase, a finite clause or a non-finite clause.

Multi-word adverbials are sometimes called adverbial phrases.

For example:-

*I ran **as quickly as I could**, but I missed the bus.*

If a whole clause acts as an adverbial, it's called an adverbial clause.

For example:-

*I'll go to bed **when the film ends.***

Adverbs

Adverbs can tell you where, when, how, why and to what extent something happens.

There are several different classes of adverb (see above).

They are often formed from adjectives or nouns by adding the suffix -ly. *For example: Quick becomes quickly, sudden becomes suddenly, intelligent becomes intelligently.*

To form an adverb from adjectives ending in *-y* change the *y* to *i* before adding the *-ly*.

For example: angry becomes angrily, busy becomes busily.

To form an adverb from adjectives ending in *-e* drop the *-e* before adding the *-ly.*

For example: feeble becomes feebly, true becomes truly.

Some adjectives ending in *-ly* need no changes.

For example: heavenly.

However there are exceptions.

For example: sly becomes slyly, shy becomes shyly.

Some adverbs do not end in -ly. *For example: fast, hard, straight.*

Articles

First the good news: There are only three articles in English: **a, an** and **the.**

There are two *types* of articles *indefinite 'a'* and *'an'* or *definite 'the'.* You also need to know when not to use an article.

The bad news is that their proper use is complex, especially when you get into the advanced use of English. Quite often you have to work it out by what *sounds* right, which can be frustrating for a learner.

Indefinite articles - a and an (determiners)

A and **an** are the indefinite articles. They refer to something not specifically known to the person you are communicating with.

A and **an** are used before nouns that introduce something or someone you have not mentioned before:-

For   "I   saw   *an*   elephant   this   morning."
example: "I ate *a* banana for lunch."

A and **an** are also used when talking about your profession:-

For   "I   am   *an*   English   teacher."
example: "I am *a* builder."

Definite Article - the (determiners)

There are two ways to pronounce "the". One "thuh" and the other "thee". To learn when we use them see the pronunciation files: How to pronounce "the".

Strong pronunciation   Weak pronunciation

You use *the* when you know that the listener knows or can work out what particular person/thing you are talking about.

For   "**The**   apple   you   ate   was   rotten."
example: "Did you lock **the** car?"

You should also use *the* when you have already mentioned the thing you are talking about.

For example: "She's got two children; a girl and a boy. The girl's eight and the boy's fourteen."

We use **the** to talk about geographical points on the globe.

For example: the North Pole, the equator

We use **the** to talk about rivers, oceans and seas

For example: the Nile, the Pacific, the English channel

We also use **the** before certain nouns when we know there is only one of a particular thing.

For example: the rain, the sun, the wind, the world, the earth, the White House etc..

However if you want to describe a particular instance of these you should use a/an.

For example: "I could hear the wind." / "There's a cold wind blowing."

"What are your plans for the future?" / "She has a promising future ahead of her."

The is also used to say that a particular person or thing being mentioned is the best, most famous, etc. In this use, 'the' is usually given strong pronunciation:

For example:

"Harry's Bar is the place to go."

"You don't mean you met the Tony Blair, do you?"

No article

We usually use no article to talk about things in general:-

Inflation is rising.

People are worried about rising crime. (Note! People generally, so no article)

You do not use an article when talking about sports.

For example:

My son plays **football.**

Tennis is expensive.

You do not use an article before uncountable nouns when talking about them generally.

For example: **Information** is important to any organisation.

Coffee is bad for you.

You do not use an article before the names of countries *except* where they indicate multiple areas or contain the words (state(s), kindom, republic, union). Kingdom, state, republic and union are nouns, so they need an article.

No article - Italy, Mexico, Bolivia, England

For example: Use the - **the** UK (United *Kingdom*), **the** USA (United *States* of America), **the** Irish *Republic*

Multiple areas! **the** Netherlands, **the** Philippines, **the** British Isles

In this chapter, we have looked at adverbials. In Chapter 6, we will look at the meaning of **Clauses.**

6

Clauses

What is a clause?
A **clause** is a part of a sentence. There are two main types: **independent** (main clauses), **dependent** (subordinate clauses).

Independent Clauses

An independent clause is a complete sentence; it contains a subject and verb and expresses a complete thought in both context and meaning. For example: *The door opened.*

Independent clauses can be joined by a coordinating conjunction to form complex or compound sentences.

Co-ordinating Conjunctions		
and	But	for
or	Nor	so

For example: Take two independent clauses and join them together with the conjunction **and**: " *The door opened.*" "*The man walked in.*" = *The door opened* **and** *the man walked in.*

51

Dependent Clauses

A dependent (subordinate) clause is part of a sentence; it contains a subject and verb but does not express a complete thought. They can make sense on their own, but, they are dependent on the rest of the sentence for context and meaning. They are usually joined to an independent clause to form a complex sentence. Dependent clauses often begin with a a subordinating conjunction or relative pronoun (see below) that makes the clause unable to stand alone.

Subordinating Conjunctions			
after	although	as	because
before	even if	even though	if
in order that	once	provided that	rather than
since	so that	than	that
though	unless	until	when
whenever	where	whereas	wherever
whether	while	why	

Relative Pronouns		
that	Which	whichever
who	Whoever	whom
whose	Whosever	whomever

For example:

*The door opened **because** the man pushed it.*

Dependent clauses can be nominal, adverbial or adjectival.

A nominal clause (noun clause) functions like a noun or noun phrase. It is a group of words containing a subject and a finite verb of its own and contains one of the following: ***that*** / ***if*** / ***whether***

For example:

- *I wondered **whether** the homework was necessary.*

Noun clauses answer questions like "who(m)?" or "what?"

An adverbial clause (adverb clause) is a word or expression in the sentence that functions as an adverb; that is, it tells you something about how the action in the verb was done. An adverbial clause is separated from the other clauses by any of the following subordinating conjunctions: ***after*** / ***although*** / ***as*** / ***because*** / ***before*** / ***if*** / ***since*** / ***that*** / ***though*** / ***till*** / ***unless*** / ***until*** / ***when*** / ***where*** / ***while***

For example:

- They will visit you ***before*** they go to the *airport*.

Adverbial clauses can also be placed before the main clause without changing the meaning.

For example:

- *Before they go to the airport,* they will visit you.

!Note - When an adverb clause introduces the sentence (as this one does), it is set off with a comma.

Adverb clauses answer questions like "when?", "where?", "why?"

An adjectival clause (adjective clause or relative clause) does the work of an adjective and describes a noun, it's usually introduced by a relative pronoun: *who | whom / whose | that | which*

For example:

- I went to the show *that was very popular.*

This kind of clause is used to provide extra information about the noun it follows. This can be to define something (a defining clause), or provide unnecessary, but interesting, added information (a non-defining clause).

For example:

- *The car that is parked in front of the gates* will be towed away. (Defining relative clause.)

Information contained in the defining relative clause is absolutely essential in order for us to be able to identify the car in question.

- My dog, *who is grey and white*, chased the postman. (Non-defining relative clause)

A non-defining relative clause is separated from the rest of the sentence by commas. If you take away the non-defining clause the basic meaning of the sentence remains intact.

For example:

- My dog chased the postman.

Adjective clauses answer questions like "which?" or "what kind of?"

Summary

An adjective clause functions as an adjective (modifies a noun or pronoun); an adverb clause functions as an adverb (describes a verb, adjective or other adverb); a noun clause is used as a noun (subject of a verb, direct object, indirect object, predicate nominative or object of the preposition).

Relative Clauses

A relative clause follows the noun it modifies. It is generally indicated by a relative pronoun at the start of the clause, although sometimes you can tell simply by word order. The choice of relative pronoun, or choice to omit one, can be affected by the following:-

Human or Non-human?

We make a distinction between an antecedent that is a human — *who(m)* — and an antecedent which is a non-human — *which*.

Who(m) is used when the antecedent is a person. **That** is used to refer to either a person or thing. **Which** is used to refer to anything except a person.

- I met a man and a woman yesterday. The woman, who had long blonde hair, was very pretty.

- The man she was with, was the man that / who won the race.

- The race was the one that I lost.

- The man, to whom the winnings were given, was with the woman who was very pretty.

Restrictive or Non-restrictive?

Restrictive relative clauses are sometimes called defining relative clauses, or identifying relative clauses. Similarly, non-restrictive relative clauses are called non-defining or non-identifying relative clauses.

In English a non-restrictive relative clause is preceded by a pause in speech or a comma in writing, unlike a restrictive clause.

For example:-

The builder, **who erects very fine houses,** *will make a large profit.* This example, with commas, contains a non-restrictive relative clause. It refers to a specific builder, and assumes we know which builder is intended. It tells us firstly about his houses, then about his profits.

The builder **who erects very fine houses** *will make a large profit.* This second example uses a restrictive relative clause. Without the commas, the sentence states that any builder who builds such houses will make a profit

In this chapter, we looked at the meaning of clauses. In Chapter 7, we will look at **prepositions**

7

Prepositions

Prepositions typically come before a noun.

For example:

- **after** class

- **at** home

- **before** Tuesday

- **in** London

- **on** fire

- **with** pleasure

A preposition usually indicates the temporal, spatial or logical relationship of its object to the rest of the sentence.

For example:

- The book is on the table.

- The book is beside the table.

- She read the book during class.

In each of the preceding sentences, a preposition locates the noun "book" in space or in time.

Prepositions are classified as simple or compound.

Simple prepositions

Simple prepositions are single word prepositions. These are all shown above.

For example:

- The book is **on** the table.

Compound prepositions

Compound prepositions are more than one word. **in between** and **because of** are prepositions made up of two words - **in front of, on behalf of** are prepositions made up of three words. For example:

- The book is in between War and Peace and The Lord of the Rings.

- The book is in front of the clock.

- The children climbed the mountain without fear.

- There was rejoicing throughout the land when the government was defeated.

- The spider crawled slowly along the banister.

In this chapter, we have looked at prepositions. In Chapter 8, it is now time to look at another important element of English Grammar, that is **Punctuation.**

8

Punctuation-Punctuation Marks

Punctuation marks are important in both written and spoken English.

In written English, the correct usage of these symbols helps to express the intended meaning of the sentence.

In spoken English, punctuation marks denote the pauses and intonations to be used when reading aloud.

Incorrect punctuation can change the meaning of a sentence.

For instance, compare the following two sentences:

Let's eat Mom.

Let's eat, Mom.

Do you see how the usage of a comma changes the entire meaning in both the sentences? The disappearance of the comma in the first sentence indicates that the speaker is asking to eat their Mom, which does not make sense. Whereas, the comma after let's eat in the second sentence helps to convey the meaning that the speaker is suggesting to their Mom to go and start eating, which sounds more sensible and also saves a life.

Symbols of Punctuation

Some of the commonly used punctuation marks are:

<u>Full Stop</u> - (.) Usually used at the end of a sentence.

<u>Question Mark</u> - (?) Usually used at the end of an interrogative sentence to form a <u>question</u>.

<u>Comma</u> - (,) Usually used to denote a pause in a sentence.

<u>Exclamation Mark</u> - (!) Used to denote shock, surprise, anger or a raised voice.

<u>Colon</u> – (:) Used to indicate what is to follow <u>next</u>

<u>Semi Colon</u> (;) Used to link two independent clauses not joined by a conjunction or used to separate two independent clauses in place of comma

<u>Apostrophe</u> - (') Used to show possession or for contraction of word.

Full Stop

The full stop or the period (.) is the strongest punctuation in the English language. It indicates, when used at the end of a sentence, a strong pause. Look at the following examples overleaf.

Let's go there.
I like this laptop.
Read this book.
I will go home.

This is the most common and obvious use of the full stop but it is also used in some other situations.

After abbreviations like etc., a.m., p.m.

After words like "Goodbye." "All right." "Hi."

Goodbye. I will see you soon.
Hi Amit. How are you?
All right. Let's finish this by Thursday.

After titles like Mr., Mrs., Dr. etc.

After decimal points like:

The sales fell by 6.3% this week.
The share market index rose by 5.1% this quarter.

An ellipsis (...) is often used to indicate a pause, an unfinished sentence or when trailing off into silence. It is also a handy tool when you're quoting and want to omit certain words.

He drank and drank...and then drank some more.

"*At the stroke of* the midnight hour, when the world sleeps, India will awake to life and freedom. A moment comes, which comes but rarely in history, ..."

Question Mark

The question mark (?) is an important part of the English language and was developed sometime around the 18th Century. Like the full stop (.), this punctuation mark is used mainly at the end of an interrogative sentence. Many people use it incorrectly or don't use it when required.

The most obvious and common use of the question mark is to end a direct question. Look at the following sentences.

Where are you going?

What is this?

Are you mad?

Is this the place?

How much is this phone for?

The question mark has other uses as well.

A. To indicate uncertainty.

He lived till 1990(?) and was buried near his house.

Gandhiji, 2nd October 1869(?) – 1948, was a great Indian leader.

B. In a series of questions.

What? He isn't coming? When did you speak to him?

He's been hospitalized? Why didn't you tell me? Is he better now?

This is your car? When did you buy this? How much did it cost?

C. To end a tag question (a statement followed by a question).

His phone was stolen, wasn't it?

She's a great painter, isn't she?

He's lost his job, hasn't he?

Many times, people use questions marks even when they're not required. One such situation would be indirect questions; these do not require a question mark.

James asked June to marry him.

The Principal asked him his name.

His father wondered whether the car was fine.

Comma

A comma is a punctuation used to denote a pause in the sentence. A comma is used to structure a sentence and helps the reader understand the meaning of the sentence.

The following are the most common usages of the comma in the English language.

1. To separate a series of words (nouns, adjectives, verbs or adverbs) in a sentence.

Philip, David, Susan and Peter went for the meeting.

Ronald is an intelligent, loyal and hardworking employee.

You must complete the assignment honestly, correctly and quickly.

Roland ran, swam and cycled to complete the athletic event.

2. To separate a series of phrases in a sentence.

Roland completed his homework, packed his bags, polished his shoes and went to sleep.

I went to the market, bought the present, got it gift wrapped and came to the birthday party.

3. To separate the parenthetical elements (a part of a sentence that can be removed without changing the meaning of the sentence).

M.S. Dhoni, India's cricket captain, hit a six to win the match.

Herbert, the headboy of the school, has been absent for the last three days.

4. To separate the quoted parts from the rest of the sentence.

The great leader told the crowd, "I will fast till death until our demands are met."

"Please go back to your houses," said the policeman to the crowd.

Exclamation Mark

The exclamation mark is a punctuation used to express strong feelings or emotions. It is commonly used after interjections or exclamations.

It is one of the most misused punctuation marks in the English language. We tend to use exclamation marks more often than what is required. The exclamation mark should be mainly used to demonstrate shock, surprise, anger or a raised voice. The following cases demonstrate correct usage of this punctuation.

Hurray!
Help!
Go away! I don't want to talk to you!
Shut Up!

In addition, the exclamation mark can also be used in very informal writing or to express irony, humour or sarcasm.

Colon and Semi-Colon

Many English speakers are uncertain about the correct usage of the colon and the semi-colon. The colon (:) is a punctuation mark consisting of two dots one over the other whereas the semi colon (;) consists of a dot above a comma.

In the majority of the cases, the colon is used to introduce a list of things while a semi colon is used to separate sentences where the conjunction has been left out.

The following examples will make the usage clear.

COLON	SEMI COLON
I have packed my cricket kit with the equipment I need: bats, gloves and pads.	Sumit likes to play cricket; Amit likes to play soccer.
A man needs three things to survive: air, water and <u>food</u>.	I drank lemonade; Manish drank tea.

The following sentence will illustrate the use of both these punctuation marks -

I talked to four men: Norman, who is from Manchester; David, who is from Brighton; Mike, who is from Hove; and Graham, who is from Ipswich.

Apostrophe

The apostrophe is an important punctuation mark in the English language which is often used incorrectly.

Here are some common incorrect usages of the apostrophe

Your's shoes are red.
I went to their's house.
The book's are on the table.
The flower's are in the vase.

The apostrophe has two distinct uses in English

Used to show possession:

Bat owned by Susan – Susan's bat
Doll owned by Susan – Susan's doll
Used to show contractions of words:
It is so hot today – It's so hot today

I have not done my homework – I haven't done my homework

Hyphens

A hyphen is a very short horizontal line between words.

Note that there is **no** space between a hyphen and the character on either side of it.

Do not confuse a hyphen (-) with a dash (-), which is longer.

The rules about hyphens are not fixed. The points below are guidelines rather than rules.

1. Use a hyphen to join words to show that their meaning is linked in some way:

- book-case (*or* bookcase)
- race-horse (*or* racehorse)
- pick-me-up

2. Use a hyphen to make compound modifiers **before** nouns:

- a blue-eyed boy (*but* The boy was blue eyed.)
- the well-known actor (*but* The actor is well known.)
- their four-year-old son (*but* Their son is four years old.)

3. Use a hyphen with certain prefixes. The prefixes *all-*, *ex-*, and *self-* usually need a hyphen:

- all-inclusive
- ex-wife
- self-control

When a prefix comes before a capitalized word, use a hyphen:

- non-English

When a prefix is capitalized, use a hyphen:

- A-frame

4. Use a hyphen when writing numbers 21 to 99, and fractions:

- twenty-one
- one hundred and sixty-five
- two-thirds

5. Use a hyphen to show that a word has been broken at the end of a line (hyphenation):

The director's requested that a more *convenient* time be arranged.

6. Use a hyphen with "suspended compounds". When we use several very similar compounds together, it may not be necessary to repeat the last part of the compound:

- They need to employ more full- and part-time staff. (*not* They need to employ more full-time and part-time staff.)

- This rule applies only to 12-, 13- and 14-year olds. (*not* This rule applies only to 12-year olds, 13-year olds and 14-year olds.)

Dash

A dash is a horizontal line that shows a pause or break in meaning, or that represents missing words or letters. Note that dashes are rather informal and should be used carefully in writing. Dashes are often used informally instead of commas, colons and brackets. A dash may or may not have a space on either side of it.

Do not confuse a dash (—) with a hyphen (-), which is shorter.

1. Use a dash to show a pause or break in meaning in the middle of a sentence:

- My brothers—Richard and John—are visiting Hanoi. *(Could use commas.)*
- In the 15th century—when of course nobody had electricity—water was often pumped by hand. *(Could use brackets.)*

2. Use a dash to show an afterthought:

- The 1st World War was supposed to be the world's last war—the war to end war.
- I attached the photo to my email—at least I hope I did!

3. Use a dash like a colon to introduce a list:

- There are three places I'll never forget—Paris, Bangkok and Hanoi.
- Don't forget to buy some food—eggs, bread, tuna and cheese.

4. Use a dash to show that letters or words are missing:

- They are really f——d up. *(Typically used for offensive words.)*
- I will look —— the children. *(Typically used in "missing word" questions.)*

In fact, there are two kinds of dash:

- the en-dash (–), which is the width of the letter "n"
- and the em-dash (—), which is the width of the letter "m"

However, the difference between them is rather technical and mainly of value to typographers. The dash is a convenient and easy mark to use in hand-writing. But it is often difficult to find on a keyboard and for this reason some people use the easier-to-find but shorter hyphen (-) when word-processing.

The slash

The slash (/) is also known as: forward slash, stroke, oblique. You should use the slash with care in formal writing.

1. A slash is often used to indicate "or":

- Dear Sir/Madam *(Sir or Madam)*
- Please press your browser's Refresh/Reload button. *(Refresh or Reload)*

- The speech will be given by President/Senator Clinton. *(President Clinton or Senator Clinton)*
- Mary will eat cake and/or fruit. *(Mary will eat cake, or Mary will eat fruit, or Mary will eat cake and fruit.)*

Do not over-use the slash to indicate "or". It can suggest laziness on the part of the writer. The "and/or" construction is widely considered to be very bad form.

2. Use a slash for fractions:

- 1/2 *(one half)*
- 2/3 *(two thirds)*
- 9/10 *(nine tenths)*

3. Use a slash to indicate "per" in measurements of speed, prices etc:

- The speed limit is 100 km/h. *(kilometres per hour)*
- He can type at 75 w/m. *(words per minute)*
- The eggs cost £3/dozen. *($3 per dozen)*
- They charge £1.50/litre for petrol. *(£1.50 per litre)*

4. People often use a slash in certain abbreviations:

- This is my a/c number. *(account)*
- John Brown, c/o Jane Green *(care of)*
- n/a *(not applicable, not available)*

5. A slash is often used in dates to separate day, month and year:

- On credit card: Expires end 10/15 *(October 2015)*

- He was born on 30/11/2007. *(30th November 2007 - BrE)*
- It was invented on 11/30/2007. *(November 30th, 2007 - AmE)*

6. The slash is used to separate parts of a website address (url) on the Internet, and to separate folders on some computer systems:

- http://www.englishclub.com/writing/punctuation-slash.htm
- file:///Users/mac/tara/photos/image.jpg

Quotation marks

We use quotation marks to show (or mark) the beginning and end of a word or phrase that is somehow special or comes from outside the text that we are writing. Quotation marks can be double ("...") or single ('...') - that is really a matter of style (but see below for more about this). Quotation marks are also called "quotes" or "inverted commas".

1. Use quotation marks around the title or name of a book, film, ship etc:

- The second most popular book of all time, "Quotations from the Works of Mao Tse-tung", has sold over 800,000,000 copies and was formerly known as "The Red Book".

Note that in the above case, we may use "italics" instead of quotation marks. So the above examples would then appear as:

- The second most popular book of all time, *Quotations from the Works of Mao Tse-tung*, has sold over 800,000,000 copies and was formerly known as *The Red Book*.
- *Titanic* is a 1997 movie directed by James Cameron about the sinking of the ship *Titanic*.

Obviously, the use of italics is not possible in handwriting or with old-style typewriters.

2. We use quotation marks around a piece of text that we are quoting or citing, usually from another source:

- In *The Cambridge Encyclopedia of The English Language*, David Crystal argues that punctuation "plays a critical role in the modern writing system".

3. Use quotation marks around dialogue or direct speech:

- It was a moonlit night. James opened the door and stepped onto the balcony, followed by Mary. They stood in silence for a few moments, looking at the moon. Then Mary turned to him and said: "Do you love me, James?"

4. Use quotation marks around a word or phrase that we see as slang or jargon:

- The police were called to a "disturbance" - which in reality was a pretty big fight.

5. Use quotation marks around a word or phrase that we want to make "special" in some way:

- Note that sometimes we use "italics" instead of quotation marks.

Double or single quotation marks?

"   "   '   '

Quotation marks can be double ("-") or single ('-'). If we want to use quotation marks inside quotation marks, then we use single inside double, or double inside single.

- He said to her: "I thought 'Titanic' was a good film."
- He said to her: 'I thought "Titanic" was a good film.'

Punctuation inside or outside final quotation mark?

If the quoted words end with a full stop, then the full stop goes inside the quotation marks. If the quoted words do not end with a full stop, then the full stop goes outside the quotation marks:

- He said: "I love you."
- She has read "War and Peace".

Note that in US English, the full stop usually goes inside the quotation marks in all cases:

- He said: "I love you."
- She has read "War and Peace."

However, US English adopts the British style for question marks and exclamation marks:

- He said: "Do you love me?"

- Have you read "War and Peace"?
- Can you imagine? He has never read "War and Peace"!

How do we indicate quotation marks when speaking?

People may say "quote, unquote" or "open quotes, close quotes" when reading aloud texts containing quotation marks:

- On page two it says, quote, Now is the time to invest, unquote.
- On page two it says, open quotes, Now is the time to invest, close quotes.

"Quote, unquote" may also be said informally in front of rather than around the quoted words:

- The brochure describes the car as, quote, unquote, total luxury.

"Quote, unquote" is sometimes used to mock or show disapproval or disbelief:

- Then he arrived with his quote, unquote new girlfriend.

People sometimes say "in quotes" (often putting up their two hands with two fingers extended on each hand, like quotation marks), indicating that the words came from another source, or in a mocking way, or suggesting that they don't quite believe what they have just said:

- Then he arrived with his new girlfriend, in quotes.

Round brackets are basically used to add extra information to a sentence. Look at these examples:

British English
() = brackets or round brackets

American English
() = parentheses

1. explain or clarify -Tony Blair (the former British prime minister) resigned from office in 2007.
2. indicate "plural or singular" -Please leave your mobile telephone(s) at the door.
3. add a personal comment- Many people love parties (I don't).
4. define abbreviations -The matter will be decided by the IOC (International Olympic Committee).

Remember that the full stop, exclamation mark or question mark goes after the final bracket (unless the brackets contain a complete sentence). Look at these examples:

- My car is in the drive (with the window open).
- I just had an accident with our new car. (Sssh! My husband doesn't know yet.)
- The weather is wonderful. (If only it were always like this!)
- The party was fantastic (as always)!
- Do you remember Johnny (my brother's friend)?
- Johnny came too. (Do you remember Johnny?) We had a great time

Square brackets or brackets

() []

We typically use square brackets when we want to modify **another person's words**. Here, we want to make it clear that the modification has been made by us, not by the original writer. For example:

> British English
> [] = square brackets
>
> American English
> [] = brackets

1. to add clarification:
   o The witness said: "He [the policeman] hit me."

2. to add information: - The two teams in the finals of the first FIFA Football World Cup were both from South America [Uruguay and Argentina].
3. to add missing words:-It is [a] good question.
4. to add editorial or authorial comment-They will **not** be present [my emphasis].
5. to modify a direct quotation-He "love[s] driving." (The original words were "I love driving.")

We also sometimes use square brackets for nesting, for example:

- Square brackets can also be nested (using square brackets [like these] inside round brackets).

Ellipsis mark ...

The ellipsis mark consists of three dots (periods). We use the ellipsis mark in place of missing words. If we intentionally omit one or more words from an original text, we replace them with an ellipsis mark. The ellipsis mark is also called a "suspension point" or "dot dot dot".

- Suppose we want to quote "The film focussed on three English learners from Asia who were studying at university." Perhaps we want to omit "from Asia who were" to save space. So we write:

  "The film focussed on three English learners...studying at university."

  The new sentence still makes sense, but the ellipsis mark shows the reader that something is missing.

We sometimes also use an ellipsis mark to indicate a pause when someone is speaking, or an unfinished sentence. Look at these examples:

- She turned to James and said, "Darling, there is something...I need to tell you. I have never felt like...like this before."
- "It's not easy to explain. It's not..." Her voice trailed away as emotion welled up within her.

In this chapter, we have looked at punctuation, which is central to English Grammar. In Chapter 9, we will take a look at **spelling.**

9

Checking your spelling

English spelling is not easy to learn. There are, of course, some rules. However, there are exceptions to these rules. Some spelling and pronunciation appear to be illogical. It is therefore very important that certain spellings are learnt.

There are 26 letters in the English alphabet. Five are vowels and the rest are consonants.

Forming words

The vowels are A,E,I,O,U. All words have to contain at least one vowel ('Y' is considered to be a vowel in words like 'rhythm' and 'psychology') **Consonants** are all the other letters that are not vowels. So that a word can be pronounced easily, vowels are placed between them. No more than three consonants can be placed together. Below are two lists. The first contains some words with three consecutive consonants and the second are words with two consecutive consonants:

(a) school, scream, chronic, Christian, through, splash.
(b) Flap, grab, occasion, commander, baggage, added.

All the words in the examples have the consonants separated by vowels.

Forming plurals

To form a plural word an 's' is usually added to a noun. There are some exceptions. If a noun ends in 'y' and there is a consonant before it, a plural is formed by changing the 'y' into an 'i' and adding '-ies':

lady = ladies
nappy = nappies
company = companies
berry = berries

If the 'y' is preceded by another vowel, an 's' only is added:

monkey = monkeys
donkey = donkeys
convey = conveys

If a noun ends in 'o' and a consonant precedes the 'o', '-es' is added to form a plural:

potato = potatoes
tomato = tomatoes
hero = heroes

If there is a vowel before the 'o' an 's' only is added:

studio = studios
zoo = zoos   patio = patios

Changing the form of a verb

When a verb ends in 'y' and it is necessary to change the tense by adding other letters, the 'y' is changed into an 'i' and 'es' or 'ed' is added:

He will *marry* her tomorrow

He was *married* yesterday

A dog likes to *bury* his bone

A dog always *buries* his bone

Using long vowels and short vowels

There is often a silent 'e' at the end of the word if the vowel is 'long':
Date, bite, hope, late, dupe.

Each of these words consists of one syllable (one unit of sound) if another is added, the 'e' is removed:
Date = dating
Bite = biting
And so on.

Adding '-ly' to adjectives

When forming an adverb from an adjective 'ly' (not ley) is added. If there is a 'y' at the end of the adjective, it must be changed to an 'i':

Adjective	Adverb
Happy	Happily
Beautiful	Beautifully
Quick	Quickly
Slow	Slowly

'I' before 'e' except after 'c'.

This rule seems to have been made to be broken. Some words keep to it but some break it. Here are some that follow the rule. All of them are pronounced 'ee' – as in 'seed':

No 'c' in front	*After 'c'*
niece	ceiling
piece	receive
grief	deceive

Exceptions to this rule are:

Neighbours, vein, either, neither, seize, weird.

Using a dictionary

Checking your spelling
Use a dictionary frequently to check your spelling. Don't guess the spelling of a word. Look it up. It is helpful to keep a list of words that you have misspelled so that you can learn them.

Looking at words
A dictionary not only tells you how to spell a word. It also tells you what part of speech the word is. Sometimes the word appears

more than once as it has different meanings and can be used as a different part of speech. Look at the following examples:

Land (noun)   (a)   The solid part of the earth
                (b)   A country

Land (verb)

(c)   To go ashore or bring a plane down to the ground

The dictionary will also often give the derivation of a word. English is a rich language that owes much to other languages. If you have time, browse through a dictionary looking at the derivation of some of the words. It can be a fascinating experience.

Making use of the Thesaurus

A thesaurus can be very useful. It will help you to find an alternative word (synonym) for a word that you have used too much. Words are shown alphabetically and beside each will be a list of words that could replace the word that you want to lose. Not all synonyms will be suitable. It depends on the context of the word.

In the next section, Chapter 10 onwards, we will build on what we have learnt in the previous chapters and look at English Language in use. We will start by looking at producing an essay followed by a story then look at producing effective business and personal letters followed by producing a CV and filling in an application form.

Practical Application of the English Language

10

Writing An Essay

Building on the lessons learnt in the previous chapters, it is now time to practice written English. We will begin by looking at producing an essay. In particular, when writing an essay or short story, good grammar and punctuation is essential.

Start at the beginning-research your essay

It is very important that you understand what is required of you when producing an essay. If you are using your own title make sure that the subject is concise and adheres to the point. Set yourself clear parameters. If you have a title given to you then make sure that you have looked at it and understand what is required of you before starting work.

It is also very important, during both the preparation and the actual writing of the essay that you stick to the title, frequently making reference to it, so that you don't wander away from the point. This is one of the most frequent problems with essay writing and, in exam situations in particular can lose you marks.

The following points should be taken into account:

- What is the title of the essay asking you to do?
- How many parts are there to the question?

- What research do you need to do? This is important. Obviously in an exam situation it is too late but it is relevant in other situations.
- Within the title of the essay what are the main points, i.e. what are the key words that you should be looking for?

Planning research

You will need to decide how and where you will do your research for your essay. The first and most obvious place would be the library, either your local library or college library. The material might be in the form of actual books but could also be in the form of archive material, such as letters, diaries and periodicals. Libraries also have archive material compiled from old newspapers and magazines. It is at this point that the expertise of the librarian will come in very useful.

You might want to interview people for your essay or visit places to gain impressions. Depending on the topic of your essay people and their memories come in very useful indeed.

Keeping records and making notes

It is important that you keep neat and logical notes of your research. Avoid keeping huge chunks of material. Inevitably you will get confused. Ensure that it is concise and can be referred to.

Bibliography

You will need to remember to keep a note of what sources you have used as you will be required to identify these. Make a note of the books that you have used stating the title, author, publisher and publication date. You may also want to enter the ISBN.

Planning your essay

After you have carried out your research you will need to start making a plan of your essay. How you are going to structure it. This is very important as there is a tendency to ramble on and lose the plot. Remember, an essay has a beginning, middle and an end. The most basic elements of any plan.

Structuring your essay

Your work will be set out in paragraphs. paragraphs define the subject matter and end one topic and start another. From the notes that you have taken, you can decide how you are going to group the main points and how the essay will flow. One thing to remember, always keep to the point and use evidence and quotations to support what you are saying.

The first paragraph of an essay will be an introductory paragraph which sets out what you are intending to do in the essay and provides a solid foundation enabling whoever is reading it to understand the subject matter. From the notes that you have taken, pick out the main points and organise them into paragraph headings. Again, this helps the flow. The concluding paragraph will sum up the essay and will demonstrate that you have achieved what it is that you set out to do.

Also remember that good grammar is crucial to a good essay. Correct spelling and punctuation. Everything that you have learnt from this book so far. I know that studying English grammar can be a little like wading through mud. However, if you keep studying then after a while it all makes sense!

Checking your essay

When you have finished the first draft of your essay you need to then carefully check the work to see if there are any spelling or punctuation errors and to delete or substitute any unsuitable words, such as words that are too long or are colloquial (unless you intended certain words to be colloquial). The following areas are important:

- Check spelling
- Check punctuation
- Are the paragraphs tidy, i.e. are they correctly indented?
- Is the language that you have used readily understandable?
- Keep to the point and keep making reference to the title
- Keep notes brief
- Make a bibliography
- Plan work carefully
- Structure your essay
- Economise on words

Sample essay title

Space travel will benefit mankind in the long run. Do you agree with this statement? Give your reasons.

****

11

Writing a story

A story, particularly a short story, contains the same principles as an essay. This is that the reader has to make ultimate sense of what it is that you are saying. You will need to plan your work, to a certain extent, and make sure that events are outlined in chronological order. In some cases you will want to carry out research in other cases not. But it must make sense to the reader.

Plotting a short story-planning the work

You will need to write down the main elements of your story in chronological order. You will need to decide where your story begins and how it will develop. Easier said than done but essential. The ending of a story is quite often the most difficult-will it lead to a predictable and inevitable end or will it have a twist-in-the-tail that surprises readers. Only you know that. The one area in which a story is very different from an essay is that you have to keep the story moving, whereas in an essay more detailed descriptions are used. This particularly the case in a short story.

Writing dialogue

Dialogue is central to a story as it can give information to the reader and can help to set the scene and help to create believable characters. Many short stories will start with dialogue, carrying the reader straight into the story itself.

Creating believable characters

This is central to any writing. If you go on a creative writing course then this is the main point that is emphasised. You should try not to have too many characters in your story as this will become confusing. remember, the reader has to grasp and hold on to the story. Too many characters can spoil the plot. You should aim to ensure that each character is distinctive so that each is given a personality and is instantly recognisable. In short stories in particular, there will be no room for detailed descriptions of their characters, so their characters have to be established by what is said by them and what the reaction of others to them is. In longer works of fiction, you can indulge in more detailed descriptions of characters, but not short stories.

Creating the plot

When you write a story you should always remember that you are writing it to entertain others. the plot is central, with characters developing within the plot. The plot should have conflict of some kind. This could be between two lovers, parent and child boss and employee, the scope is enormous. But it should be kept simple. Whereas for a longer work of fiction you can have a sub-plot, in a short story you cannot as there is generally not enough room to develop this area.

The first sentence

The introduction to your story is crucial. The first sentence has to grip the reader and make him or her want to read on. This is the essence of all fiction. If the first sentence is dull and boring the reader will switch off. So spend time on the opening lines.

Proof reading and editing a story

When you have finished the story, proof read it for errors and for grammar and punctuation. **Good grammar and punctuation** are the tools of the author and as you go through what you have written this is the opportunity to tighten up by deleting words or changing sentence construction.

The following are the key points to remember when editing work:

- Check spelling
- Check punctuation
- check dialogue-have you begun dialogue with a new paragraph?
- have you kept to the same tense throughout-chopping and changing tenses can confuse the reader?
- have you kept to the same 'person' throughout- i.e. first person, third person?
- Is the language accessible-is it free of repetition? Colloquialism should be avoided.

Sample short story

Taking into account what has been written above, plan the outline and produce the opening paragraph of a short story based on: **the burning car.**

12

Writing letters

In this chapter, we will look at writing an effective letter. Depending on the letter, and to whom it is directed, the use of good grammar is crucial in conveying your message. In this chapter, we will look at writing business and personal letters.

Business letters-Aiming your letter

Letters project images of you and your organisation to the broad outside world. Clients and general customers of your business will build up a picture of you and your organisation from the style of letter that you write.

When you write a letter you should consider to whom you are addressing it. What is the aim of your letter? A clear aim will tell the reader what he or she wishes to know, but also helps you as a writer by telling you what you do not need to write.

A letter provides a permanent record of transactions between organisations. That record will guide future actions and may also appear as evidence in cases where contractual problems are arising and court action is necessary. Your record must be clear and correct. Ask why you are writing and then you can focus on what your letter is aiming to achieve:

- payment of an overdue account
- sales of a new product
- technical information
- confirmation of a meeting

Who is your reader?

You should give thought to the person who will read your letter. For incoming letters seek guidance from:

- the name of the job or department title at the end
- the content of the letter

If you are initiating correspondence, make sure that you have targeted your reader accurately. It might be worth making a telephone call to ask who deals with a certain area. Once you have done this you can direct your request to the most appropriate person. Buyer and salesman have a different outlook on a similar product. In making a technical enquiry to the buyer you will expect a competent reply: the salesman's competence may direct you to the benefit of buying the product.

One very important point is that the level of your writing must be your natural way of expressing your meaning. If you try to adopt any other style than the one that is natural to you, you will emerge as strained and unnatural.

What does your reader need?

When you respond to a letter, take a close look at what it requires:

- Is it looking for information?
- Does it need action?
- What action does it require and by when?

Consider how to approach the task

Writing acts as a window through which the reader may see the personality that lies behind the words. In certain cases, this can be a disadvantage, for example if you have an indifferent attitude or if other factors have influenced your mood. This will be reflected in the letter. You have to remember that when people read letters they will pick up varied messages, depending on their own personality and your mood and style when writing the letter.

There are advantages. Once you are aware that your attitude shows in your writing then you can use this to considerable effect. Do not try to hide your personality, let the reader see that you are able to understand the readers problems, that you are willing to help or that you are patient if a mistake has been made or incomplete information has been given.

Your approach will obviously vary considerably depending on who you are writing to. If you are writing to complain about poor service you will expect to be firm in your tone. You are likely to be plain speaking, specifying what is wrong and laying out timescales for action. If you are writing in reply to a complaint from a customer, a firm approach will be inappropriate. You will need to adopt a different, more conciliatory approach.

In professional firms, letters rarely go beyond the conventional picture of three short paragraphs. These letters may be:

- offering advice of some sort, such as financial advice
- specifying an architects detailed requirements for progress on a job

In handling more extended material you will need a more complete and visible classification of the content. This will show in headings, and perhaps sub-headings within the narrative, to give the required direction to the reader.

Decide where and when to write

The place and timing of your letter is critical. The reader will not be very happy if your letter arrives on the morning that a crucial decision has to be made, a decision which will be influenced by your letter. Neither will that person be happy if the letter goes to the wrong address. This can easily happen where businesses are organised around different addresses. Your sales letter must arrive at the time that relates to the budget, or the buying decision. At the same time it must be persuasive enough to encourage the reader to put it on record in anticipation of such a time.

Planning and structuring a letter

Many people who write letters do so in a hurry and will not give a great amount of time or thought to the contents. In some cases, this may be suitable, especially if you are writing a very short letter of acknowledgement. However, in longer business letters that require more elaboration, then this is not appropriate and a great deal more thought needs to be exercised.

A relatively small amount of time is needed to plan and write letters and, in the long run, will save you time and effort. A well-planned letter will ensure that you communicate the right amount of information and detail to the reader.

Many writers sometimes have problems with the opening sentence of a letter. There is the idea that the opening sentence is of the utmost importance and that the rest will flow easily. This is not always the case. When planning a letter, work from the general to the particular. The detail will then tend to fall naturally into place.

The contents of your letter

When determining the content of your letter, you should ask yourself:
- who is my reader?
- What does that person need to know?

If that person needs to know very little, for example that you intend to be at a meeting, a few words will suffice. However, if the person wishes to know quite a lot then you will need to be very methodical in planning the contents of the letter.

When approaching such a task:

- gather relevant information
- allocate the information to main sections
- give each main section a heading

Decide the sequence of delivery

It is difficult to think about the content of your letter without giving thought to the sequence in which you will deliver it. A natural order will quite often emerge.

When you are resolving a problem:

- what has gone wrong
- why it went wrong
- what will we do to put it right

When you review activity:
- what we have done in the past
- how we operate currently
- what we plan for the future

A natural order promotes a logical flow of thinking and allows the letter to end at the point you wish to reach:

- looking ahead rather than looking back
- solving a problem rather than raising one

For more complicated letters people tend to group their material functionally but find the sequence more challenging and often repeat material.

To plan your sequence:

- spread your headings across the top of a sheet of A4 using the landscape or horizontal plane.
- List the points that relate to each heading in columns
- Consider any changes in the sequence
- Decide whether larger sections should break down into sub-headings or whether additional headings would be better.

An outline classification can show your intended approach to a colleague or other. Changes are easy to make and the outline classification will serve as an excellent prompt for your draft letter.

Forming paragraph structure

There are no rules for paragraphing that require text to be broken after a certain number of words or line. Paragraphs have a lot more to do with consistency of thought than length. However, there are guidelines that help to convert planned content into readable paragraphs:

- change paragraph with each change of subject
- if your subject requires lengthy exploration, break it into further paragraphs that reflect the different aspects.
- Headline your paragraph to give an early indication of your subject.

Many business letters are brief and to the point and can be delivered in a single paragraph. The key is to ensure that the reader can follow your train of thought and that your letter is not one long rambling monologue.

Many single page business letters appear in a three-paragraph format that reflects:
- identification
- explanation
- action

In these cases the opening and closing paragraphs are often short – commonly a single sentence. The middle paragraph expands to the extent that it is necessary to complete.

Paragraph length is also about a particular writing style. A single sentence can make an emphatic paragraph but over-use of single sentence paragraphs will diminish their effect.

Control your sentence length

Writers struggling to construct a sentence are usually concerned with finding the right words to convey their intended meaning to the reader. You should avoid the long lead-in to a sentence. Your lead-in should be snappy and direct as opposed to long winded. If you find it difficult to express your thoughts you should think to yourself, what exactly am I trying to say?

Researchers have measured writing to see what makes it readable. Answers usually include the types of words used and the sentence length. The ideal sentence length is usually about twenty words. After this a sentence can tend to become unwieldy.

Words are not just counted between full stops: the colon and semi-colon also determine the sentence structure for this purpose.

You should remember that you are seeking a readable average sentence length: you are not trying to make every sentence twenty words long. Variety in sentence length will produce a more interesting style. You should adopt a conversational approach in your writing, controlling your sentence length.

Use a range of punctuation

Again, in chapter 8, we looked at punctuation generally. Relating this directly to letter writing, the trend is to use only the punctuation you need to reveal your meaning.

Layout of letters

Letters always have a certain convention that distinguishes them from e-mail and memorandum. Letters always begin 'Dear...........' and end 'Yours sincerely.........'. This is the same whatever the nature and tone of the letter, whether you are writing a strong letter of complaint or a more measured letter.

However, letters have become less formal and word processing now gives many more options for the alignment and appearance of text than a layout that was once dictated by the limitations of a typewriter.

The majority of letters are left aligned only, leaving a ragged right margin that appears less formal and aids reading. Key information such as the reference, date, address, salutation, complimentary close and enclosures is increasingly aligned to the left margin.

Letterheads have changed too. Once upon a time, all information appeared at the top of the page. Now you may see the company logo prominent at the top but much of the statutory detail at the foot.

Quote references in full

We put a reference on a letter so that when someone replies quoting the reference, we are easily able to find the letter on file. Always quote a reference when replying. Much correspondence is stored electronically and the quoted reference may be the only manageable way of retrieving a particular letter.

One common layout will begin:

Reference
Date
Address of reader
. . . .
. . . .

An alternative layout will show:

Address of reader   Your ref:
                                     Our ref:
. . . .   Date:
. . . .
. . . .

In the second example, the information will often appear in print on the company letterhead and the position will reflect the letter template on the word processor.

You should look at the address not simply to direct your letter to the receiving organisation but to the individual from whom you seek a response. It is now usual practice to include the name and job title of the recipient as part of the address. As that information appears through the window of the envelope your information can be targeted unopened to the reader.

Choose an appropriate salutation

Try to include the name in the salutation at the start of your letter. This will:

- get commitment from a reader whom you have targeted precisely
- set a personal tone for your writing

Writers sometimes identify themselves with just name and initials at the end of a letter. However, there is a practical problem in that we need to attach a style (Mr Mrs Miss Ms) to the reply.

Very formal style still appears in business letters. You may find a letter that begins:

For the attention of Mrs D Smith

Dear Sirs

We acknowledge receipt of your recent letter...............

A name allows you to be more natural and direct:

Dear Mrs Smith

Thank you for………..

You will need a formal salutation when you write to an institution rather than a named reader.

A PLC or a limited company is a single legal entity and it is logical to address the company as Dear Sir. Avoid writing Dear Sir/Madam. Whichever part of that generalisation applies to it, it is offensive for its failure to relate properly to you. A general name can make a good alternative.

Use informative headings

Most letters will benefit from a heading. This serves to:

- tell the reader what you are writing about
- provides a descriptive reminder of the content of a letter you may later wish to retrieve.

In an extensive letter distinguish between a heading that covers the broad scope of the letter at the start:

Pullfir Contracts
Annual check J.Peters
Training programme

And the more specific headings that occur at intervals to identify the specific topics of the letter.

In a short letter you may write predominantly on one topic but then wish to make a small unrelated point later. This need produces clichés like:

May I take this opportunity to remind.............

While you are right to take the opportunity you will make a clear case by putting your thought under a separate heading. The letter will take on the following form:
Salutation
Heading one
....
....
....
Heading Two
....
Close

Think about the sequence in which you handle your headings. Where possible end with the topic that needs action.

Bullet points form a practical sub-structure for letters. They are best for items that require separate identification but which need no specific reference.

Before we can authorise a mortgage we will require:

- three payslips
- your P60
- proof of residence.

A sub-structure of numbers is helpful where you wish to raise a number of points which require a specific answer from your reader.

Summary and sample business letters.

Before laying out sample business letters it is important to summarise these points:

- Aim your letter carefully. You should ask yourself why you are writing and who is your intended recipient. What does your reader need?

- Make sure you plan and structure your letter and decide the sequence of delivery. Take pains to ensure that your punctuation is correct and also control your sentence length.

Sample business letters

(See overleaf)

Introducing your firm

PRINTING SERVICES LIMITED

Mr D Davies
Askews Castle Ltd
42 Smiths Drive
Aberdeen
Perthshire
Scotland
321

38 King Road
London E17 4PT

Tel: 020 8123 5467

Our ref:

21ˢᵗ July 2013

Dear Mr Davies

I am writing to introduce my company to you. We are a business that provides printing services, consultancy and printing machinery to companies in the north of England. Our clients include Nobles, Bloomsbury and Polestar Wheaton Limited. In particular we offer:

- Cost effective printing solutions to meet all requirements.
- Consultancy services. These are designed to ascertain a clients needs.
- Follow up work with recommendations and costing.

At this stage, we enclose our latest brochure for your perusal. If you are interested in our products and services either now or in the future, please call me on my direct line 020 8123 5467. We would be pleased to supply further details on request or to discuss your requirements further.

Yours sincerely

David Askew
Sales manager

Offering new products
PRINTING SERVICES LIMITED

Mr D Davies   38 King Road
Askews Castle Ltd   London E17 9PT
42 Smiths Drive
Aberdeen   Tel: 020 8123 5467
Perthshire
Scotland

1st July 2013.

Dear Mr Davies

We are pleased to introduce the latest addition to our fast expanding range of printing presses, the Digital plus reproduction unit. This innovative product is the latest in a line of presses introduced by Printing Services Limited. It is designed to enable small publishers to cut costs and keep their stock holdings down. There are tow distinctive features that distinguishes our press from others:

- Low print runs of 1 or more can be achieved.
- The press can achieve a two-week turnaround from placing of the order to fulfilment.

For a limited period, we are making a special offer available exclusively to our customers:

A 10% discount off the normal trade price for each press ordered.

We enclose sales literature for the press. To take advantage of this offer please ring me direct on 020 8123 5467. Please note that this offer is for a limited period. We look forward to receiving your call.
Yours sincerely

David Askew
Sales Manager

Chasing a reluctant buyer

PRINTING SERVICES LIMITED

Mr D Davies   38 King Road
Askews Castle Limited   London E17 9PT
42 Smith Drive
Aberdeen   Tel: 020 8123 5467
Perthshire
Scotland   Ref: 123

24th July 2013.

Dear Mr Davies

We were delighted to receive your enquiry about our printing press last week. I understand that you expressed interest following a demonstration by our agent. We were sure that you would be impressed with the press and would appreciate the advantages to your company.

We can confirm that this product is still available at a 10% discount to you. However, we have to point out once again that this offer can extend for a limited period only as we have received many expressions of interests and resultant firm sales.

I am pleased to enclose our sales literature for your further perusal and information. Please do not hesitate to contact me to discuss the purchase of our press.

We look forward to hearing from you again.

Yours sincerely

David Askew
Sales manager

The three letters above demonstrate all of the key aims of a business letter. The letter is aimed at the key person, the message is clear. There is a clear understanding of what the reader needs. The letter is planned, structured and the sequence of delivery leaves the reader in no doubt as to the message.

The sentences are short, crisp and to the point. The reader will be very clear about the intent and will be impressed by the layout.

There are many varieties of business letters but the key themes are exactly the same throughout.

Writing personal letters

So far, we have concentrated on the nature and form of business letters. These letters, by their nature, require a great deal of attention to detail as they act primarily as records of business and need to be specific in their aim.

Personal letters, whilst also ideally needing the same level of knowledge of the English language and attention to detail, have a different starting point. This is that they are personal and are often written to people we know and have conversed with many times. Therefore, many elements that we need to be aware of in business letters, such as the avoidance of jargon and clichés, are quite often present in personal letters.

Nevertheless, there are certain formal conventions that need to be observed at the outset.

Personal salutations

The personal letter will differ from the business letter in that you will usually put your name and address on the top right hand side, as with the example overleaf and the date under the address.

The letter will, in many cases, be handwritten, to add to the feeling of intimacy, and will finish not with 'Yours sincerely' but quite often will finish with 'love, or 'regards' or even 'cheers', depending on who you are writing to and how you have written the letter.

See example letter overleaf.

Example personal letter.

38 Cromwell Road
Walthamstow
London E17 9JN

3rd May 2013

Dear Peter

It was really great to see you at the opening match of the world cup last Wednesday. Hey, what a great game wasn't it? I really loved the first half and, although the second half dragged a bit there was loads of action.

Did you see Stanley Peters? What a real snake in the grass! He was excellent in the first half but was real lazy in the second. He should have been substituted.

Anyway, enough about football. What about you and your family? I hope that you are all faring well and Susan is OK. She is a really nice person and you have a very good partner there.

Well, old buddy, enough said. Once again, it was really great to see you and I look forward to the next time. We should get together a little earlier and maybe have a pint or two, just like old times. We wont overdo it, as we used to, but it would still be a nice break.

Cheers
Dave

As you can see, this letter is full of the elements that have been advised against in a business letter. This is precisely because personal letters are personal and you are often talking to people with whom you have built up a relationship over the years. You know and understand the person and the type of language that is acceptable, therefore the use of clichés, jargon and so on is perfectly acceptable.

In many ways, the personal letter is the opposite of the business letter in that, in the business letter, you are trying to portray a positive image, well constructed and to the point with the express aim of communicating your message in a formal way.

You would certainly never handwrite a business letter, or finish by saying 'cheers'.

In some cases, with a personal letter, you may wish to adopt a mix of formal and personal. If you were writing to your Uncle Tom, who you have not seen for twenty years, you would not be writing in a very chummy style and yet you would not be over-personal either. You would use some elements of intimacy connected with the family and family memories but you would also be looking to present a rather formal image as you do not know this person well enough to adopt a chummy approach.

The art and craft of writing personal letters very much depends on you as a person, the person you are communicating to and also what you are trying to say. If you are in correspondence with a friend or acquaintance who is interested in politics and you are discussing political events then you would probably need to be well versed in the language and grammar, as well as current affairs, to be able to express yourself effectively.

If you are discussing matters of the heart then you would need to be possessed of a language and style that allowed you to express yourself sensitively. In many cases, the advantage of knowing the English language, and the ability to express your self, bringing into play all the elements of language, such as grammar and punctuation, will prove to be a great asset. It is hoped that the brief introduction contained within this book will assist that process.

Editing and proof reading

Editing and proofreading letters is perhaps one of the most important elements in the production of effective letters, whether business or personal. An effective editor/proof reader will need a range of skills, including a sound knowledge of the English language and of the intricacies of grammar. This book has, hopefully, allowed the reader to absorb the basic structure of the language. You should always allow time for proof reading and understand that the task is part of the process of producing a letter.

13

Putting Together a Workable CV, Filling In An Application Form.

In this chapter, we will look at the art of putting together a workable CV and also filling in application forms. Drawing on what you have learnt so far in the book, including presentation, you should be in a position to create a CV. There are certain key points to consider when formulating a CV.

Fundamental requirements of a CV

The letters "CV" stand for Curriculum Vitae, which derives from Latin. Translated, this means "the way your life has run". Correspondingly, the CV is a personal statement, which demonstrates to the employer the way your life has run. The CV will usually start from your early education and progress through to higher education and chronicle your employment. It will also chronicle your personal interests. The end product should present a well-rounded picture of you.

A CV serves several basic requirements. Firstly, it highlights your potential value to an employer. It also provides a framework within which an interview can be guided and acts as a record of the interview, or its substance.

The layout of the ideal CV

Before any information has been entered onto the CV, consideration needs to be given to the layout. By layout, I mean the actual design of the visual presentation. Remember that a better impression will be made if the person reading the CV feels comfortable with what they are reading. Effective visual design reflects neatness, and the end product should be easy on the eyes and immediately give an impression of orderliness, which will go a long way to impress the reader.

Although final recruitment decisions are not made on visual presentation alone, as opposed to content, the way information is assembled makes an important first impression and could mean the difference between someone bothering to spend time with your CV or deciding to move on to the next one.

Make sure also when you are typing the information that you use all of the features of the Word Processor (assuming that you are using a WP). Make sure that you have clean margins and that you are consistent when presenting your information. For example, you might want to ensure that your work is not right hand justified as this lends a certain uniformity to a CV. Maybe it is better to leave it unjustified or "ragged right" as it is known.

Quality

Obviously the quality of a CV depends very much on the way it is laid out and the information contained within it. However, it is also true to say that a much better impression is made with a quality paper. There are different qualities and thickness of paper and I would recommend that a thicker more durable paper be used, such as Conqueror. A good quality paper at the outset enhances the effort that you will make when laying out information and presenting yourself in the best light.

Style

By style, I am referring to the way you present information about yourself. Remember that there are two important rules underlying any form of presentation

Be brief and be clear! You do not want to bore the reader by going on and on, using twenty words when five will do. However, conversely, you do not want to be too brief and exclude the main emphasis of what you wish to get across.

Writing the ideal CV is a skilled business and requires thought and concentration, along with creative editing. If possible, I would advise showing the finished product to someone skilled in the art of report writing before you send it to a prospective employer.

The basic structure

Although the basic structure of a CV is well known, it is more important to structure the CV in a way that shows you in the best light.

The traditional structure of a CV is as follows (see overleaf):

Name
Address
Occupation
Telephone number (landline and mobile)
Email
Date of birth
Place of birth
Marital status
Next of kin
Health
Driving license
Religion (if applicable)
National insurance number
(Sometimes religion, nationality and passport number if applying for a job abroad)
Secondary education
Higher education
Professional qualifications
Employment history
Other (interests, achievements etc.)

There are several variants on this approach. Remember, what you are doing is delivering information to the potential employer. This person might well be interested in your employment history at the outset and it may be more effective to deliver this information right at the beginning. Leave the matter of details such as date of birth and secondary education until the end and begin with the most important first. Therefore, instead of adopting the traditional approach you might want to use the following format:

Name
Address
Telephone number
Email
Career
Achievements
Professional qualifications
Education
Interests
Other personal details
Date of birth

We have considered the most important aspects of the ideal CV. These are quality, style and layout. Finally, there is the content. These initial pointers should enable you to begin to put together your first CV.

Example of a complete CV'.

The following is an example of a typical CV. You should include and exclude information depending on the perceived requirements of the employer. For example, it may not be necessary to include religion or location or other facts. This depends entirely on the employer.

See overleaf.

Example CV

PERSONAL DETAILS

Full Name:	Rupert James
Occupation:	Computer Scientist
Address:	92 Faversham Street
Telephone Number:	012396789
Mobile	98767545321
Email	info@straightforwardco.co.uk
Date of Birth:	5-3-75
Place of Birth:	Rich Street Ninetown Anywhere
Nationality:	British
Religion:	Buddhist
Marital Status:	Married with son aged 7
Next of Kin:	Mrs James address as above
National ins no:	123456789
Driving License:	Current full
Passport Number:	456789
Health:	Excellent
Preferred location:	Anywhere at all

Education, Training and Qualifications

Education: 1986 - 1993

Northampton Grammar School
GCE Passes:

English	Grade	(d)
Biology		(c)
French		(c)
Physics		(b)
Economics		(b)

Higher Education

1993 - 1996 Waldesley Polytechnic, High Street,
Waldesley Northampton
BA   Computer Sciences: Pass with distinction
Year One: Computer Theory
Year Two   Advanced Computer Theory
      "   Computer Trainee on placement,
                  ElectronicsSystems Ltd,
                  Long Road, Northampton.
                  Assisting the Chief Engineer
                  developing computer systems

Year Three: Applied Computing

Short Courses
Authentic Electronics Limited September 2004 Fault finding on
Computers (2days)
October   2004   Software Analysis (1 week)
December 2004   Advanced Spreadsheets (1 week)

Professional Association

Royal Institute of Computers
Fellow of the Institute May 2004

CAREER HISTORY

August 2004 - current.
Authentic Computers, Northampton. Consultant
In this post, I am acting in the capacity of consultant to the
private and public sectors, advising on systems usage. I am

employing the technical know how gained in my previous jobs. I am conversant with most computer packages

Salary: £25,000 Per Annum

September 2001 - July 2004
London Borough of Shepwhich. Senior Computer Manager

In this post, I had responsibility for overseeing a change in the authority's computer system. This involved carrying out systems analysis and producing a brief for the council, who subsequently accepted the brief and instructed the computer department to effect the change.

After two years I was promoted from Computer Manager to Senior Computer Manager.

Whilst employed by The London Borough of Shepwhich I obtained the status of Fellow of the Royal Institute of Computer Scientists. My main duties for the company were to oversee the development of a computer system for a local authority. This involved giving technical advice to the authority and supervising a workforce of 23 people who were directly involved in the installation of the equipment. During this time, I gained experience of the following packages:

Wing 1 - Wing 2 - Super Wing-Wing for Windows

September 1999 - August 2001
I took two years out from work to fulfill ambition to travel around the world with my wife.

Personal Interests

I am interested in squash, badminton and indoor football. In addition, I am interested in studying history and Science. I enjoy walking in the countryside and swimming. I also like to participate in the community and am on the local conservation committee. I speak French and German fluently and have traveled to these countries for my current employer on business.

Health

Excellent

Preferred location

London

Application forms

Not all jobs want you to send in a CV. If you are applying for a job that requires you to fill an application form in, there are several important rules to remember. When you receive the form never fill in the original in the first instance. You might make a mistake and not be happy with what you have written and might need to start again. By then, if you are using the original, it will be too late. Always copy the form and fill it in with a pencil. This way, you will not suffer if you make a mistake.

Application forms can either be written or typed. It is up to you to exercise your discretion at this point. However, only if your handwriting is neat should you fill in the form by hand. A typewritten form will be more immediately readable and make a better first impression. Send the application form in with a brief covering letter. Do not falsify the application form, as this will form part of your contract of employment when offered the post.

The job application should be treated much the same way as your CV. As discussed, when you interpret the job advertisement you need to analyze the nature of the job before compiling the CV. You should do exactly the same with an application form. The first task is to read the job description that should normally accompany the application form.

It is absolutely essential that you understand the requirements of the post. Many organizations will send a person specification that outlines the essential and desirable criteria, which the applicant must meet before he or she is considered for the post. Although the essential criteria are the most important, if those short listing for the post have a number of good candidates then they will revert to the desirable criteria as a way of further eliminating candidates.

It follows that, when completing an application form, which has a person specification in it, then you should fill in the application carefully following the requirements of the post, ensuring that you meet the essential and desirable criteria. In addition to essential and desirable criteria, there will be a skills required section, which will generally outline the skills and abilities, which the person must demonstrate.

Make sure that when you fill in your application form that you follow the person specification closely, you have read and understood the job description and that you comply with all the requirements. If you do not, then you are wasting your time.

Normally, there is a space on an application form, which asks you to outline your experience to date and to demonstrate why you want the job. You should be concise and to the point. On too many application forms, applicants really go to town in this section, producing a whole life history amounting to many sides of paper. This is totally unnecessary and will, more often that not, result in your application being thrown in the bin.

You should follow carefully the requirements of the post, from the person specification to the job description, and lay out clearly and concisely your experience to date. You should then relate this to the job on offer and explain why you think that you are the ideal candidate.

If there is no job description or person specification to work from, then you will need to read very carefully the requirements of the post from the advertisement, and then construct what you think are the main aspects of the job related to your own experience. In this way, you can present the interviewer with a picture of yourself. It is not very often these days that an application form is not accompanied by a job description.

If you feel that you are on uncertain ground, for example when faced with filling in an application form without a job description or person specification, then you might want to contact the company concerned and request further information.

Content of application forms

The application form will proceed on a logical progressive basis, much as a CV is compiled. The form will start by asking you your name and address, some will ask your date of birth. The type of organization that you are applying to will very much determine the application you are being asked to fill in.

Some application forms are designed with great care and reflect the ethos of the organization, such as omitting to ask certain information on an equal opportunities ground. For example, some organizations deliberately do not ask for information relating to age as this is thought to affect the perceptions of those who are short listing for the post.

There will be a space for a phone number. This is important, as the company may want to contact you by phone shortly after the interview to discuss the possibilities of offering you a job.

Other details at the beginning of an application form might be sex, marital status and country and place of birth. This again will vary depending on the organization you are applying to. The next section of the form will ask you for details of education. You should start with your most recent job first. However, it is very important to read the application form as it might state otherwise.

Applications might ask for salary information and reasons for leaving the post. On a CV it is not wise to volunteer this information, with the exception of final salary. However, some application forms may require this and will say so.

If the state of your health has not involved disability but has involved long periods off work then you should try to demonstrate to your employer that this problem is now in the past and that this will not affect your future employment.

Most applications end by asking for references. These will normally be from your current employer and one other, such as someone who has known you for a long time. If you are not currently employed then the reference should be from your ex-employer. Make sure that you know what your employer or ex employer is going to say about you in advance. It follows that you should let this person know that you are going to use them as a reference.

Many employers do not bother taking up references despite asking for them. Others always take them up as a matter of course. Some applications state that they will take up references when a candidate is short-listed. You should contact the company and state that you do not want this ads it could affect your relationship with your employer (if this is the case).

If you have not yet been employed then you should use school or academic references. A second reference might be a personal reference. Some applications will ask specifically for a personal reference. In this case, it is better to use a professional reference, i.e. someone with whom you have worked in a voluntary capacity or even someone you have worked in a paid capacity for.

There are a number of other questions that may appear on an application form, such as whether or not you have a driving license or whether you speak any other languages. Notice periods, possible start dates and periods of notice, plus membership of professional bodies may also appear. There may also be a requirement to outline your ambitions. Be careful and tailor this to your employer's requirements.

Finally, remember that good grammar, accurate spelling and punctuation will go a long way to help you get that job. Once again, apply everything that you learnt from the first section of the book.

Good luck!

Glossary of terms

Acronym. A word formed from the initial letters of other words.

Adjective. A word that describes a noun

Adverb. A word that qualifies a verb, an adjective or another adverb.

Articles. The a, an

Clause, dependant. A group of words containing a verb that depends on the main clause. they cannot stand alone.

Clause, main. A group of words that contain both a subject and a verb and make sense by themselves.

Conjunction. A word that links two clauses together.

Gerund. A present participle used as a noun.

Homophones. Words that are pronounced the same but spelt differently and have different meanings.

Inverted commas. Speech marks put around speech and quotations.

Noun-abstract. A word that denotes a quality or state.

Noun-collective A singular word which refers to a group of people or things.

Noun-concrete. The name of a thing.

Noun-proper. the name of a person or place. It always begins with a capital letter.

Paragraph. A group of sentences dealing with the same topic.

Phrase. A group of words not necessarily containing a verb or making sense on its own.

Preposition. A word that governs a noun or a pronoun.

Prose. Written language in sentences or paragraphs.

Simile. A comparison of two things using 'like' or 'as'.

Synonym. A word that can be used to replace another.

Thesaurus. A collection of synonyms.

Verb, intransitive. A verb that is not followed by an object.

Verb, irregular. A verb that does not follow the usual pattern.

Verb, transitive. A verb that is followed by an object.

Index